SINCERELY SPEAKING

WHY WOMEN CHEAT
(AS REVEALED BY WOMEN)

PART OF THE ASHA SERIES

JORGENSEN E. DIMOJI

PublishAmerica
Baltimore

First printing

All characters in this book are fictitious, and any resemblance to real persons, living or dead, is coincidental.

PublishAmerica has allowed this work to remain exactly as the author intended, verbatim, without editorial input.

ISBN: 978-1-4489-6202-0
PUBLISHED BY PUBLISHAMERICA, LLLP
www.publishamerica.com
Baltimore

Printed in the United States of America

Dedication

This book is dedicated to all the accused, betrayed and lonely women wherever they maybe.

ACKNOWLEDGEMENT

I thank my family and friends for their support and encouragement. And God, The All Knowing.

 INTRODUCTION

Men and women cheat for different reasons. In the past however it was a rare, almost something unheard of— women cheating on their spouses but because things have fallen apart in relationships all over the world this has become the order of the day in societies world wide. Interestingly however these days more and more women are becoming guilty of cheating on their men and they have a wide range of reasons for doing so.

The issue of why spouses cheat on each other is a thorny problem that faces many couples today in all countries, communities and societies. We all are witnesses to the break down of values in most societies today and that is why everywhere you go or wherever you maybe—United States, Britain, France, Russia, Iraq or in a remote village in Nigeria or India the same problem is very much prevalent. Thus for every and any reasons peoples' feelings or emotions are being hurt by supposedly loved ones—husbands, wives, boy friends or girl friends. As a result couples have become forever hurt when they find out that their "better halves" have been unfaithful on account of the deep level of intimacy and affection involved in these relationships. In other words being a victim of unfaithfulness is very stressful and causes a lot of pain which may eventually lead to a separation, divorce and in some extreme insane cases murder or suicide. This is the case because love, passion, affection, emotions or feelings have no boundaries, color or creed. A Black woman will be hurt as much as a White or Hispanic woman whose spouse has been unfaithful. It is very clear here that it does not matter who is involved in the soured relationship be him or her black, white, Indian, Nigerian, Chinese, Mexican. It is of no significance because somewhere in New York, Lagos, London, Ihube—Okigwe or Indonesia hearts are being broken every hour on the hour and once upon a time happy families are being destroyed by what is happening in relationships between spouses.

In certain situations when relationships hit the rocks the consequences are sometimes very devastating not only to the couples or families involved but also to the society as a whole.

For a long time men have always viewed and used women as their "escape goat" to cover up their shortcomings, hide their weaknesses and explain away their failures. As far as men are concerned women are solely responsible for the alarming rates of infidelity and failed relationships. This according to the men has its' roots in the biblical garden of Eden when the first man,

Adam blamed his falling out of favor with God on his mate Eve, accusing her of passing on the supposedly "fruit" of life to him that eventually led to their being driven out of the garden of Eden. Since ancient times also men have blamed all their woes, trials, tribulations and temptations from and of the devil on women. In this light it becomes a lot easier and fashionable for a man to call for example his cheating ex—wife all kinds of derogatory names than it is for him to admit that maybe his ex-wifecheated on him because he had no time for her in his schedule because he spends most or all of his time with his buddies at the club, watching sports all day everyday and doing every other thing else but his spouse.

Men have even gone so far as calling women very disrespectful and derogatory names such as bitches, tramps, freaks and hoos that tend to debase and offend women and all in their concerted efforts to continue to maintain their claim that women are responsible for all their troubles especially infidelity and failed relationships.Men are also quick to remind everyone of the many important, powerful and influential men in history and in contemporary times who had met their waterloo at the hands of the women in their lives—from "Mighty' Sampson and Delilah in the bible to President Bill Clinton and Monica Lewinsky in the United States. This trend of blaming women for all their problems and shortcomings which began centuries ago has continued till this very time. In all countries, communities and societies all around the world this "game" is still being played out by men who try to stick it on the women anytime when things do notgo right while presenting and representing themselves as "saints" and angels and seeing themselves as 'philosopher kings' who do not and cannot do any wrong.

Coming out swinging women in their defense argue that it is rather the opposite. They fiercely contend that it is men that are responsible for the numerous break ups among couples or spouses. The women to a certain degree however do accept that they sometimes cheat on their spouses but unequivocally heap the whole blame on the men in their lives arguing that they have been forced into being unfaithful to their mates because of the actions and inactions of their men .In other words the women are saying' yes we do sometimes cheat on our spouses but we are justified because of a number of reasons and all attributed to their spouses. Further more women claim that they are not as promiscuous or always as 'horny' as their men counterpart who they confidently argue are more inclined to cheat and pounce on any available thing just to get their 'nod" off, arguing that women have more self control and respect for themselves than men who they describe as "scavengers" and "dogs" that are unable to control their ever raging libido which they aptly describe as always "hot and ready' to eat or be eaten.

As far as the women are concerned men cheat because to them, men are nothingbutpigs.In their further response to the charge leveled against them by the men as being solely responsible fro the many break ups in relationships, women argue that men oftentimes mistake or misjudge their submissive nature, their respect, their obedience, their loyalty, their admiration and affection for them for granted and as a sign of weakness. They are of the strong view that men always feel it is acceptable for them to run the streets and do whatever that pleases them and at anytime and any place of their choosing while women must "check in" with them first before they could do a thing and they definitely do not find this funny. To add salt to injury women claim that men after all their misbehaving always turn around and blame women when things go wrong. This hurts them so much when they are so treated and subsequently accused of wrong doing by men. This the women contend is the real issue when they are so treated and betrayed by the men who always claim with their lying tongues how much they love their women. To the women this is a very bitter pill to swallow and when they are so treated by men who claim they love them, and are often times left very distraught by such state of affairs. This situation in some cases have resulted in some very serious consequences one of which is cheating on their spouses. This is because at this point the women have had enough and will begin to seek ways to get even with their cheating partners.

In all this craziness happening all over the world with relationships breaking down almost as soon as they were cultivated as in failed or failing marriages or relationship, womenare simply saying that although they sometimes do cheat on their spouses, they however seriously argue they do so because often times they have been pushed or forced into doing so because their spouses have left them with no other choice than to seek and get a pay back on their cheating, always not available and sometimes abusive spouses by sleeping with other people too, men and or women alike as the case maybe." It doesn't even matter anymore' as they often say.

In this book different women from divergent backgrounds and age honestly bare their minds on this very thorny issue. Let's read their stories and share their experiences which they hope will support their claim that it is the men in their lives that drive them into infidelity. Girls too wanna have some fun. When girls talk. Let's hear it from the girls.

Ms Cecil Parker
vs.
Warren Derrick—
"Sleeping with step-daughter"

Ms Cecil Parker and her husband Warren Derrick have been married for almost twenty years and their marriage blessed with six children, two girls and four boys. A very hard working woman, Ms Parker did not really care much that her husband for all these many years that they have been together did not have a job and accordingly continued rather happily to provide for their family without any complaints or bitterness. Even on special occasions such as Christmas, Easter, Valentine's day, fathers' day, sweetest day or on his birth day, Ms Parker always spoil him by showering him with very expensive gifts and special treats. In fact Ms Parker did everything for husband believing very strongly that he too loved her just the same way she loved, cared and provided for him but little did she know that her husband for almost two decades and blessed with six beautiful children has been cheating on her for many years, almost immediately after they got married.

However the "wall' in their once upon a time very happy and successful union came crashing down when she found out that her heartthrob, her darling, her soul mate, her man, her beloved husband has been sleeping with their twenty one year old step-daughter "from his wife's previous relationship) since she was sixteen years old. This was a shocker and a very rude awakening for Ms Parker who had devoted almost her entire lifetime and resources on the man she thought she knew and loved.

Ms Parker couldn't believe what she had just found out about her husband and her heart was broken beyond repair if you will. Disappointed, dismayed, disgraced and devastated Ms Parker after a long period of reflection and soul searching finally decided it was time for her to move on and leave what had happened behind her. Accordingly she stepped out to find a peace of mind and a shoulder to cry on and the only available way for her to begin the process of healing for her was to get even with her cheating, lying and unappreciative husband and this she boldly accomplished by cheating on her husband with their best man at their wedding which subsequently let her gate wide open for anyone willing to come in. This eventually led to the break up of their once famed relationship as Ms Parker moved out of their once shared happy home and moved on with her life but this time not with just one man in her life but many, as many as were willing to give she was willing to receive .

Ms. Lineal Williams vs. Greg Mack— " Caught with girlfriend's mother"

Ms. Lineal Williams, a very pretty young lady was deeply in love with her childhood heart throb Mack. They have been together as a couple for the past eight years and everything seemed to be going pretty well for the young couple. In fact their love for each other was so strong and tight that they are rarely apart from one another, always doing things together to the envy of many who looked up to them as an example to imitate or copy. Meanwhile the young couple at this very time were leaving in Ms Williams's mother's home. At first everything was good, nice and quiet as they all wined, dined and danced together, happy and satisfied with each other and one another.

However after a few months had passed by since her boy friend moved with her and her mother, Ms Williams began to observe some notable changes in their relationship. At first Ms Williams didn't take it to be anything very serious or something to worry about and as such she didn't really pay much attention to seeming new developments in her relationship with her boy friend Mack and went on about her business as usual. Even all efforts and outright warnings by her very close friends regarding what themselves were seeing and observing especially the very cozy relationship that her boy friend and her mother were having fell on deaf ears. Ms Williams just didn't want to hear it and would not even entertain any thoughts that her Mack was cheating on her with anyone how much more her own mother.

However it wasn't too long before things started to take a turn for the ugly after her close friends succeeded in getting her to listen and pay attention to what was going on between her boy friend and her mother. On their prodding she decided to set up a trap or sting operation to either confirm or deny all that she has been hearing concerning her boy friend and her mother having their own relationship on the side if you will. And boy it worked.

This was how it went down according to Ms Williams. On this blessed day Ms Williams had informed her man and her mother that she was going to the hair salon to get her hair and toe nails done after which she will then go the grocery store to get some food for the house. In all she was going to be gone for at least two or three hours or maybe more while leaving her mother and her boy friend home alone all by themselves. However rather than going to the hair salon and the grocery store as she had made them to believe, Ms Williams instead quietly sneaked into one of her neighbor's home, less than three minutes walking distance from the home she shared with her mother and boy friend Mack and waited with her heart beating so fast.

After waiting, wondering and worrying for about sixty or so minutes Ms Williams decided it was about time for her to take perhaps the most important and difficult walk in her entire lifetime back to her home for better or for worse. Ms Williams didn't have the patience to walk but rather sprinted back to her home and when she opened the door she was shocked beyond all belief by the sight of what was unfolding before her very own eyes as she caught her boy friend Mack having sex with her mother in her bed room and on her bed. Having been hit so hard by what she had just witnessed Ms Williams lost it and passed right out right there and then and was rushed to the emergency where the doctors and nurses were able to revive her.

On leaving the hospital and getting home from the hospital after her very terrible ordeal Ms Williams refused all plea for forgiveness from her boy friend and her mother but proceed to take her own pound of flesh too on both her mother and her cheating boy friend. The consequence was that the once Ms congeniality, the very amiable Ms Williams turned into a monster overnight literally. She was so devastated to the extent that she began to sleep with just anyone available in the "hood' which unfortunately led to her untimely death having contracted the dreaded HIV virus while having sex with all manner of men out of her frustration and a heavy sense and feeling of betrayal by her boy friend and her very own mother. And the girl died. Unsung.

Ms. Kysha Parry

vs.

Jay Robinson—

"Cheating with girlfriend's

best friend"

Young and pretty Ms. Kysha Parry was highly distraught on discovering that her eighteen year old childhood sweet heart Jay was cheating on her. To make matters worse Jay has been sleeping with her girl friend's best friend Jewel and this is how the whole thing went down in the words of Ms Parry. Both youngsters had known each other since their pre-teen years as early as when they were eight and nine years old respectively, that is Ms Kysha and Jay Ms. Parry's parents had moved from their home town Chicago, Illinois to Detroit, Michigan where they had met Jay and his parents who were their very close neighbors. After settling down in their new place of residence in Detroit and became acquaintances with their new neighbors, it didn't take a long time for both Ms Kysha and Jay to find each other and became very close friends. The occasion that kind of brough all this about was at Jay's 10th birthday party at his parent' home. Since they got together which was cemented at his birth day party, the two love birds have remained inseparable ever. By the time they got into their middle teenage years it was crystal clear to both parents and others that these tow youngsters were deeply in love and when they turned sixteen and seventeen years old, they took their love story to another level by moving in together as a couple.

Meanwhile Kysha who is not really the out going type and not as gregarious as her boy friend Jay had little few friend but has one very special friend, Amanda, both of whom have been friends since their kindergarten years. The story was that it was either that Ms Parry was with Jay, her boyfriend or Amanda, her best friend at any point. Her life seemed to have revolved around her boy friend Jay and best friend, Amanda.

It is no wonder then that Ms Parry was shocked beyond belief what she had witnessed one inglorious winter evening when she caught her man, Jay having sex in their bedroom with her best friend, Amanda. Although very hurt and devastated Ms Parry nonetheless because of the love and deep affection she had for Jay tried to forgive him and work towards rebuilding their relationship. This was not easy on her and despite all efforts to let go all that had happened she just could've through with this betrayal. It was a very difficult pill to swallow and having failed in her efforts to forgive and put the incident behind her, Ms Parry decided it was time for her to move on and began to seek for a shoulder to cry on, someone to lean on.

On account of the huge disappointed, betrayal and humiliation she had suffered because of her boy friend's infidelity, especially cheating on her with her childhood best friend, she swore never again in her young life to have anything whatsoever to do with a man, any man in her young life and beyond. At last poor young Ms Parry finally found love and peace of mind in the arms, heart and warm embrace of another woman, Tina, her ex-boy friend's younger sister who became her new lesbian lover . Thus ended her once flourishing relationship with Jay who betrayed her trust by cheating on her with her childhood best friend Amanda.

Anita Menendez
vs.
Jersey James—
"Wife's half sister and a baby"

Ms Anita Menendez had fallen in love with the man who later became her husband since they were both teenagers. They loved each other so dearly so it seemed and after years of just being friends they got together and took their relationship to the next level by getting married on valentines day hoping to live together happily ever after. However their fledging marriage came to a sudden and shocking halt after almost twelve years of marriage. According to Ms Menendez she was shocked to the bones when she found out that her husband has not only been cheating on her for many years with her step sister but has a four years old child, a baby girl with her step sister, Nadia.

Meanwhile the couple didn't have any children in their many years of marriage and this made it a little bit easier on Ms Menendez to move on with her life after such a deep betrayal by her husband. Highly devastated she moved out of the home she once happily shared with her cheating husband and found her own place. Though on her own at this time Ms Menendez still couldn't let go or forget her ugly experience with her ex-husband. She finally became seriously depressed and in her efforts to find happiness she completely became a new person, very much different from who she used to be. She began to sleep with different men in her elusive search for a peace of mind from the humiliation and betrayal she had suffered in the hands of her ex-husband, Jersey. Ms Menendez is still looking for a shoulder to lean on even as I write.

KIMBERLY EVANS
VS.
KENNY—
" ALWAYS GONE,
MISSING IN ACTION"

Although aged forty seven, Ms Kimberly didn't look anything her age and if you met her and she tells you she was twenty nine years old you would not even raise an eyebrow. Ms Evans is also a very good looking, beautiful and attractive woman who any man willwant to have but she had found the love of her life in Kenny, her boy friend for about nineteen years who she had met when she was twenty eight years old. They were happy and everything seemed to be going on alright with the couple except that Kenny her man was the jealous type of a guy and wouldn't give her a breathing space, always scotching her to death with his many everyday questioning of her "who's that on the phone" "what you looking at" " why are you late" "where were you at" "what took you so long" "who you with" and all that kind of stuff. His constant harassment of hcr finally made her to quit her job and stayed at home all day every day while Kenny, her boyfriend went to work. And he had no problem with this and actually was happy with the situation because that was what he had wanted from the get go.

Kenny, a workaholic had two regular jobs(9-5), a weekend job and a hustle going on the side doing home repairs and fixing cars. Kenny was always on the go, from one job to the other, on the roof somewhere, painting or doing some drywall somewhere, anywhere and was never at home to be with his girl. He was always gone chasing after money,bread as he fondly refers to it and had a lot of it. He was paid as they say and with his money he provided Kimberly with any and whatever she wanted or desired. Whatever it is cars, clothing, jewelries, over seas trips and expensive vacations. Whatever, she had it.

In spite of all these Kimberly remained a very unhappy woman because the only thing she really cared about deep in her heart, her man Kenny was missing in her life. He was always gone when Kimberly needed his companion-ship, his affection and his love. He was missing in action chasing after money and had little or no time for her lady Ms Kimberly. This situation continued without any noticeable changes despite all that she did to make her man to at least pay her a little attention by spending just a little quality time with her and show her some affection, some loving, if you will. After many futile efforts to make her man come to his senses Kimberly finally was fed up with the whole situation and decided to take steps to take her life back.

Meanwhile while all this drama was unfolding in her relationship with her boy friend, she had kept one very special friend who she confided in concerning the problem she was having with her man. This very special friend was Reggie, Kenny's best friend. It was in his arms that Kimberly sought and found solace and what she had lacked from her boy friend, Kenny. Not only was Reggie available any and all the time Kimberly wanted him, he was also hot and ready. Kimberly loved it all and felt like a virgin once again both in spirit and in truth. And that was how Kimberly got her groove back.

Tracy Steel vs. Mike—
"Three other women, three different children"

Tracy Steel was married for over twenty years with the man she thought was a "God sent". Their union was blessed with five children, two girls and three boys. Ms Steel had a great job working in a big auto industry in one of the Mid Western states and her husband too had a good job working for one of the computer giants as a Soft Ware Manager. They had everything they ever wanted and sent their children to the best schools around and life was good and well. Ms Steel loved and adored her husband so much and showered him with love and affection and believed he loved her too. All this time however little did she know that her husband of over twenty years has been cheaing on her almost from the very day they became husband and wife and all the time they have been together as a married couple. While Ms Steel was busy loving her man unconditionally and without any restraints he on the other hand was occupied with caring and loving other women. Even when rumors started flying around and finally got to Ms Steel concerning her husband's philandering Ms Steel always rejected any and every such suggestions . In fact in one incident she got into a physical confrontation with one of her family members who tried to convince her to see the light and end her relationship with

Mike because of his infidelity to her. After this fight her family and friends swore never to have anything to say to her again in life about her marriage to Mike and their fears were confirmed in a few weeks later because it did not take long before Ms Steel found out what her husband has been doing all these years they have been together. She not only confirmed that her husband has been unfaithful to her all these many years but discovered to her utter chagrain and total shock that Mike, her husband also had three other children outside wedlock and from three different women.

Furious, angry, devastated, betrayed and humiliated Ms Steel after many days of crying and weeks of depression and soul searching decided to seek her pound of flesh from her cheating husband because she was unable to deal with the situation as it were. In this regard she turned her life around fast and became a completely different human being.

She was so distraught to the point that she began doing things and engaging in activities she had previously rejected and denounced. She started to drink heavily, smoke cigarettes and doing all kinds of illegal drugs such as weed, crack cocain and heroine. Ms Steel unlike her former self became an over night whore sleeping around with just anyone from the neighborhhod and surrounding areas including her husband's family members . And another good girl gone wild.

Kimberly Davis
vs.
Aaron Rod—
"Insecurity and jealousy"

Kimberly Davis is a very beautiful middle aged woman who has been married to her husband for seventeen years. Blessed with two children, a boy and a girl and very affluent, this couple had the good life going on for them except for one thing that would never go away . She was always being accused by her husband of cheating on him.

According to Kimberly at the early part of their marriage things were pretty good. This was the period before they had their children. She confessed that her husband loved, respected and treated her very nicely and as such they really didn't have any serious problems or issues between them. Things however started to change when the couple stopped having children and like a curse her once beloved husband of so many years had suddenly turned into something else becoming a nightmare to her almost over night. He literally became an "animal" always filled with anger against her and right from the blues her husband began to accuse her of cheating on him with several different men utter chagrin.

When this all started Kimberly initially didn't take it seriously thinking that her husband was merely joking with her or "trying to figure her out" and hoped that it was going to stop just as fast as it had began. She was mistaken because Aaron her husband instead of slowing down with his very wide accusations against her rather escalated it y constantly harassing, embarrassing and hounding her morning, afternoon and night with questions of her unfaithfulness. Through all these Kimberly remained peaceful, praying and hoping that things would get back the way they used to be between her and her husband. To her disappointment things never did get any better between them but rather went from bad to worse. The climax came one inglorious morning when her husband grabbed her by her neck and gave her the beating of her life as she was about to leave the house for work.

That was it.

Kimberly has had enough and decided it was time to do something about it and filled with anger and frustration she got her "pay back" on her husband when she started seeing other men one of which was Tony, her husband's best friend and best man at their wedding.

Linda Spears
vs.
Mark—
" Always broke,
do nothing boyfriend"

Ms Linda and her boy friend Mark loved each other so much and have been together for five good years. On the surface it seemed as though they both loved each other but underneath, their relationship all these years has been a rocky one, one that could best be described as a "roller-coaster" relationship but nonetheless they hung in there. Although it was evident that both loved each other but there was something that was missing that almost all the time tried to break up their relationship. They had no money and were living from "hand to mouth" which was always a source of argument between them but they held on believing and hoping that "love will conquer all".

You see Linda had no real job but did bring some money home from doing other peoples' hair at a booth she was renting from a lady from her church who owns a hair salon few blocks from their home. Mark her boy friend on the other hand had no job or any reliable source of income and was not bringing in any real money home for the up keep of his home. All he did was run the streets and the neighborhoods with his boys all day every day. All pleas by her girl friend Linda to him to try and get a job or a hustle going on so as to help with the family fell on deaf ears. They nonetheless continued to leave together anyway and soon Linda became pregnant with their first child.

All through her nine months pregnancy Linda continued to work very hard every day to provide for her home. Eventually when her child was born their responsibilities increased also because now they not only have to provide for themselves but also for the new baby, clothing, toys, medical care and all that. At this point one would expect Mark her boy friend to step up to the play and be a man by taking responsibility as the man who was good enough to make the baby but he didn't. Instead he continued his street life and poor Linda was left alone to provide for herself and their new child and because she loved him she continued to be with him but also continued to ask him to get a job so that he can help her out but as usual Mark didn't pay her no mind and continued living his life the way he wanted .

Now left with no other real choice, Linda to stay alive and well and be able to provide for her new baby decided it was time and right for her to do what she had to do for the sake of her new baby and this she did by any means necessary. Linda started to not only cheat on Mark but actually engaged in prostitution to provide for herself and her innocent precious new child.

Kathy Coleman
vs.
Matt Gilmore—
"Very disrespectful, arrogant and violent"

In her own account Ms Coleman recounted how she was betrayed and almost destroyed emotionally by her spouse who she claimed never cheated on her but she instead has been cheating on him but blamed it all on his boy friend Matt.

Ms Coleman in her story recalled how her boy friend was always and forever talking down on her, cursing her out without any provocation, disrespecting her in the presence of other people and making her seem worthless by calling her all kinds of derogatory names—"freak, hoo, fat, ugly and making her feel and think she's a nobody, almost " a good for nothing type of sister" if you will.

Ms Coleman confessed that not only was her boyfriend very disrespectful to her, he was also very abusive and violent towards her and recalled one day she would for ever like to forget when she was beaten black and blue by her man for no other reason than just talking back to him when he wouldn't stop cursing her out before his friends and family members. He ran their home with a very heavy hand, dishing out orders and expect compliance without any questions or comments, whatever, anything.

All these made her loose her self esteem and self worth and to recover herself and take back her life Ms Coleman found other ways to find an emotional connection and balance somewhere else and ended up in the arms of different men looking for love and someone who will love her for her, someone to uplift her and not tear her down. Her true soul mate.

CYNTHIA CRAIG
VS.
REGGIE BOLDIN
"ONE MINUTE MAN"

Twenty year old beautiful Cynthia Craig was convinced beyond all doubts that when she found the love of her life, Reggie, 27 that she would never have any reason in the world to worry about sex, that is being satisfied sex wise, if you will, in her relationship with her boy friend Reggie. That being the case at least she had thought, there would not be the temptation or lure of looking out elsewhere for sexual satisfaction. She was pretty sure of getting it from her "Big" Reggie when she wants it, how she wants it and where she wants it. However this was not to be as herdreams of a wonderful and exciting times with her Reggie soon began to show some crack because she was shocked and highly disappointed that her man was quite the oppossite of all she had thought and hoped he was, Mr Macho, Macho man. The result of this revelation was was not too good for their once flourishing relationship because it eventually led to their breaking up as a couple.

Hey don't be too quick to blame Cynthia yet because her 6ft 8inches and 232 ibs boy friend was a non performer especially against the backdrop of his very athletic built, his young age and all this other stuff which rightly led Cynthia to not only believe that he was the "bom" but excitingly was looking forward to an encounter. When the opportunity finally came through for both of them she disappointedly discovered that her "Samson" was just a piece of pie. He was no good, I mean no good in bed. He was a "one minute" man, always screaming and "coming" like crazy and dripping all over the place just on the first few thrusts and nothing more than sixty seconds, just a minute before his girl was barely bent over. Big Reggie with all his might and power was not good in bed and was not taking care of business as he should thus leaving his girl friend highly unsatisfied and wanting and pleading for some more which her boy friend never was able to do. He was nothing more than just a "one minute man" who always busts a "nod" almost immediately as got to doing it or pretending to be doing it, whatever.

Poor Cynthia because she loved him so much and would love to preserve thie relationship tried all she could to make her man "stand up" and "step up to the play" by making her feel like a real woman by letting her have it a lot longer,when and how she wants it hard and longer until maybe they both "come" and not just always only him. Not giving up she searched the internet all night and day, read several medical journals and books,sought counsel from close friends and family members, consulted sex experts and counselors, sought medical advice and bought all kinds of sex enhancement drugs like Viagra, Cialis all in her committed efforts to save their relationship. Sadly though all her efforts did not produce any positive results and their situation did not get any better but got worse.

Having failed in her efforts to make her man be the real man that he was to and now convinced beyond any iota of doubts that her man was "no good", Cynthia who incidentally was a "horny" bee her self decided that enough was enough and decided it was time for her to get her groove back by getting some, "some something something" and so went all out to get her some of the "good stuff" she has been missing all the time she has been together with Big Reggie. You bet. She didn't have to wait too loong or look too far to find her "dig' because all the while all this was happening between her and her boy friend, eagerly waiting on the wings was Randy, her boy friends cousin who didn't hesitate to get "cracking" with Cynthia at the very first time Cynthia finally "rolled" her eyes and hip at his direction one Sunday afternoon, indicating to him and inviting him "in" . Thus beginning with Randy her life was to change for ever as she began seeing different several men and started hanging out at the different local bars and always on the go, jumping form one vehicle to another all because the man she loved woefully failed her by not taking care of his first responsibility to her, sexing her so good and make her enjoy her woman hood. Eventually their relationship ended and both former lovers parted their different ways to chart a new course for themselves for better or for worse.

Julia Smith
vs.
Eric Cleveland—
"Too old school"

Always dressed up like a young teenage girl—tight fitted jeans, short or mini skirts and other provocative outfits and flaunting what she's been blessed with, a good sized breast, well curved hip and her very much talked about butt Julia felt very confident of herself and regarded herself as part of the new generation, the so called "new school".

Although not all that young at thirty eight years old, pretty and vivacious Julia saw herself as a very 'hot mama" and very well believed that at 6ft 2 inches tall and having the built of a Super model, she felt great about herself and always boasted that she could have any man she ever wanted, any time, any place and when ever. Eventually she fell deeply in love with Eric who she had met at the club a couple weeks back. After a few going out and hanging out together they both decided to get together as a couple and a relationship was born.

In the beginning it was all good and nice as everything was fallen in place—a good home, great jobs and very nice cars, they seemed to have the world in their pockets and the world under their feet. Howver this was not to last a long time because it simply tore apart almost as soon as it had started. The reason for this new state of affairs as usual was the issue of sex or the sex "thing".

Her new man Eric in his middle 40's belongs to the "old School" and acted like one in all his dealings and you can tell by the way he does his things, like for example his way of dressing and the types of clothings he has, his music choices or preferences, the way he talks and even the way he walks, everythin. A very much lay back individual, Eric was a direct opposite of his very sensous and vivacious woman. In all this Julia didn't care much because all she really wanted from her man was very good and satisfying sex sessions involving a whole lot of the new generation sex acts than just having her woman lay down and spread her har legs wide open and letting him get in between her things. It is a different story these days and times especially to the new generation or new school who almost all of the times would want to do "nasty"—eating it or going down town on that "monkey" like you eating French Fries or Macaroni and cheese and licking that monkey like an Ice cream cone, "spanking that ass", "sucking them breasts till the nipples turn red and hard, sucking them feet clean and the man having his brains sucked out by the girl and those other good stuff before "getting down" to the point. Eric wasn't having none of that and refused to do any of them.

Julia tried everything she could to get her man Eric to

change wearing very sleezy and sexy lingerie from Victorai Secrets, setting the mood right in their bed room by lighting up all kinds of different "mood" candle lights, changing the color and quality of their bed room windows and drwing the blinds down, giving the room a very sensual dim background and of course always butt naked with no clothes on at every opportunity she and Eric were alone together at home and even purchasing a couple of sex toys and stuff.

All this she did to get him excited and in the mood to rumble good and hard but "shoo" nothing happened, nothing changed as good boy Eric remained the same good old Eric.Nothing could get him to change and start giving her woman what she really craved for like licking her ass, eating her pussy good, playing with her "teddy" and massaging her back, neck and all over." Hell no" Eric consistently told his woman.

Having exhausted all her tricks and efforts and nothing seemed to be working out good and yearning to have her "groove" back, Julia eventually started cheating on her man which finally led to the break up of their relationship only after a few months. When it was all said and done Julia ended up moving out of the home they once shared together and found fulfilment in the arms and warm embrace of their next door neighbor while Eric moved on perhaps to find an equally "old school" soul mate. Gingerely.

Conclusion

As some of the cases discussed in the book have shown loneliness is one of the major reasons why women cheat on their spouses. Women who are involved in relationships that are not emotionally fulfilling are more likely to cheat on their men. In general women who are in unsatisfactory marriages or relationships often feel lonely, left alone all by themselves and if a woman is not getting the attention she feels she deserves in a relationship there is the likelihood that she maybe tempted to seek that attention elsewhere and become involved in an affair. A spouse who is always preoccupied with his job, business or hobby may end up not having enough quality time to share or spend with his partner. This often results with the woman consumed with the feeling of loneliness, being left alone or abandoned if you will, and this feeling of loneliness can drive a woman to cheat on her husband or spouse. Women need attention from their men.

At this point we can then safely conclude that lack of attention to one's spouse or mate is a very dangerous thing in any relationship. I do not really care how much you claim or "mouth" your love and affection for your spouse but doe's not spend reasonable time with your spouse. I tell you, it is not going to work . You all are going to have a problem because sooner or later things will begin to fall apart between the two of you whether you like it or not.

Human beings by nature love attention and love to be pampered especially the women folk. Humans also love, cherish and want affection and when these things are lacking in any relationship the consequences are often disastrous. This is not very hard to understand because lack of attention and by extension lack of affection for one's partner causes a deep feeling of loneliness, low self esteem and self rejection which ultimately may bringabout a separation or detachment both emotionally and physically. Therefore love, affection and companionship are very key ingredients in any relationship because they help to maintain stability in relationships until perhaps "till death". In this regard therefore couples involved in relationships must ensure that each partner fulfils his or her roles and are advised never to take things for granted hoping that things will work themselves out because in most cases they don't work that way. In other words solid and stable relationships are not and cannot be left to happenchance.

Enduring relationships are sustained by the actions and inactions of the two people involved in the relationship. Good and lasting relationships demand hard work, commitment and dedication from both spouses and there is no better place to demonstrate how hard anyone can work than in your relationship with your spouse. The alternative to not working hard to ensure a stable and enduring relationship between spouses is a break up of the relationship and its' attendant conquences.

It makes a lot of sense to sometimes give people especially those we claim we love or are in love with the benefit of the doubt. That is to say in other words couples must learn and cultivate the habit of trusting each other because it is almost impossible to maintain any stable, happy and enduring relationship when spouses don't trust one another even to the minimum degree. This is one of the major reasons relationships are tearing down all over the place as it has become increasingly difficult for many couples to trust each other.

Granted that our world today has radically changed from what it used to be because of technology and other advancements in human development which has resulted in the erosion and decimation of societal values, I am still of the strong view that there are still out there good and honest men and women who can still be trusted and depended on and who are still very much committed to cultivating and maintaining very strong, healthy and enduring relationships. These are men and women of high integrity whose yes are yes and no is no. These are people who speak and stand on the truth no matter what.

Spouses must cease to quickly rush to judgement of each other and as a consequence take actions that may lead to the break up of relationships. Rather they should trust each other and listen to one another patiently even when things don't go right or when there are suspicions or doubts in their relationship for example spouses must not let their jealousy or insecurity becloud their sense of judgement when dealing with each other and trusting one another is the key.

Love is a sweet thing. Love is great but no matter how good, sweet, deep and "blind" love might be it comes with a price. In other words being in loved or being loved carries a a burden, a responsibility on both spouses in love. This burden or responsibility is the contribution that each spouse has to make to ensure a stable and happy relationship. I disagree with those who say relationships should be like 60/40, 80/20 or 70/30.

Relationships should and must be 50/50 between spouses and rightly so because in any relationship partners must bear equal burden of both the good, the bad and the ugly.

It is a trasversity of natural justice nonetheless for a man, any man no matter his culture, color or creed to sit back and relax while expecting and sometimes even demand that his spouse become the bread winner in the home. Any man who is not capable of providing for his woman and family is unworthy of a man.

However gone are the good(?) old days when the man is looked upon to shoulder all the responsibilities in relationships. Both couples must work together as a formidable team and pull together to build and sustain their relationship. In the long run however any man who is lazy and unable to provide for his woman and household must be prepared to deal or cope with the consequences of his actions or inactions as the story of Ms Linda Spears and Mark perfectly illustrated.

Finally in any relationship spouses must always strive not to be too quick to blame one another for their failures. Rather they should encourage and support each other to find out why for instance cheating or being unfaithful to each other occurred in the first place.

Maybe when couples honestly do this they might discover the path or the role each one of them played in pushing the other to cheat and maybe figure out ways to make the necessary or needed corrections or adjustments in their relationships and perhaps go beyond their fears and misunderstandings and push forward together. Perhaps forever.

When Girls Talk.